ANVIL NEW POETS 3

ANVIL NEW POETS 3

edited by

Roddy Lumsden
& Hamish Ironside

ANVIL PRESS POETRY

Published in 2001
by Anvil Press Poetry Ltd
Neptune House 70 Royal Hill London SE10 8RF

This book is published with financial assistance
from The Arts Council of England

Designed and set in Monotype Ehrhardt by Anvil
Printed and bound in England
by Cromwell Press, Trowbridge, Wiltshire

ISBN 0 85646 283 7

A catalogue record for this book
is available from the British Library

Contents

TABISH KHAIR

KONA MACPHEE

ROBERT SEATTER

Preface

IN THE PAST seven years, Britain's commercial poetry lists
have produced, between them, less than a dozen debut col-
lections. In a changing market, though poetry is selling
much better than has been reported, it is increasingly
difficult to get published for the first time. The Society of
Authors' Eric Gregory awards are still an invaluable way
of bringing forth young poets and the independent poetry
publishers do publish a handful of newcomers, but tend to
lose the more successful ones to the commercial lists.
Anthologies of new poets are still a good way of showcasing
emerging talent and, looking back at Faber's late
Introduction series, Carcanet's *New Poetries* and the *New
Poets* series from Chatto and Anvil, one often finds the early
work of some of our best-known poets. In editing this
anthology, we follow on from the fine work done by Graham
Fawcett and Carol Ann Duffy on *Anvil New Poets* 1 and 2.
Both editors tracked down a fine clutch of poets including
Mimi Khalvati, Richard Price, Gerard Woodward, Alice
Oswald, Colette Bryce and Kate Clanchy.

The ten poets in this book were selected by Peter Jay and
by us. Some had sent work to Anvil, others were known to
us or recommended by others. We considered well over a
hundred poets and had a difficult time reducing the shortlist
of thirty or so to the ten included. Looking through the
manuscripts, we were surprised by how much good poetry
there is – competent, well-written, thoughtful work – but
how little of the work was truly striking and fresh. Too many
manuscripts smelt of the exercise workshop and too many
seemed to say the same things about the same subjects. We
think the poets here show originality and promise and we
hope and expect that many of them will go on to publish fine
first collections, with Anvil or elsewhere.

RODDY LUMSDEN

A NEW VOLUME of poetry by a contemporary poet will be doing well if it sells more than five hundred copies in its first year. A typical work of local history, say, or book of crosswords will generally sell a good deal better than this. This goes some way towards explaining why so few collections by new poets appear: most of them lose the publisher money. For the commercial presses, poetry is, to some degree, a loss-leader, while the independent presses such as Anvil can only survive thanks to funding from the Arts Council or elsewhere. In my estimation, the proportion of poetry manuscripts that reach publication, other than by self-publishing, is perhaps less than one in a thousand. That new poets can make their way at all is due in large part to the continuing survival of magazines such as *The Rialto*, *The North*, *Thumbscrew*, *Smiths Knoll* and *Acumen*.

Some of the poets in this anthology were discovered in magazines such as these, or through readings, workshops and recommendations. Others were found among the daily deluge of unsolicited manuscripts. Reading through these hundreds of manuscripts, it was easy to lose sight of quite what one was excited by in poetry in the first place. One can find oneself boredly impressed with a good technician or clever writer; they are somehow more wearying than plainly bad poets. I found myself stopping once in a while to read Glyn Maxwell's 'The Ginger-Haired in Heaven' or Edward Thomas's 'Wind and Mist' to remind myself of exactly what poetry is capable of.

My criterion in selecting poets and poems for this anthology was to choose those works which came closest to reaching the qualities of poems such as these. Reviewing the poems through the editing process, I became more certain that we had succeeded in this. These are poems that not only stand up to repeated readings, but actually improve with each.

HAMISH IRONSIDE

RICHARD ARONOWITZ

Born in 1970, Richard Aronowitz grew up in rural Gloucestershire. He studied Modern Languages at Durham and Heidelberg and Art History at the Courtauld in London. He works as Head of Research for Impressionist and Modern Art at Sotheby's in London.

Aronowitz's poems have two distinct voices. In some, such as 'Anatomy of a Liar' and 'Foetal Position' in the present selection, an ironical tone is skilfully combined with rhythmical pace and dense musical effects. Aronowitz is also at home in a quieter, more reflective poem, less immediately striking but perhaps ultimately more rewarding. Examples of this include 'Midnight in Midwinter on Midsummer Common', with its particularly fine first stanza, and the understated pathos of 'Gastroenterology'.

Prelude

After the winding cadence
of the road,
we climb the five-bar gate,
printing each stave
with a semiquaver of leaf-mould
and loose grit
from the shattered tarmac.
A pheasant in the field
shrills in alarm
at our approach,
its colours like sunrise
against a canopy
of evening-shaded trees;
skeletons in the closet
of a summer behind us now –
under an unbreakable lock,
turning from a major
to a minor key.

Foetal Position

This is where I come in:
the snap of rubber, the slap of skin,
the ten-inch box to put me in. Forceps
flex like anorexic can-can girls;

a midwife checks her watch as I fail to hurl
a first cry at unregistered walls. My umbilicus
twists like an eel kept in the dark
about the likes of you; the stark

staring light arcs a gloss on mucus. That slick
on the sheets will come out in the wash,
that prick of the needle's silenced by the cosh
of codeine; mouthwash swallows the taste of fear.

You incinerate the palest ghost of a chance
that I may return to haunt your dance,
interrupt your life's smooth sentence. Well,
I am gone. Tell me am I wrong?

Gastroenterology

They weigh you in like a wrestler
going into the ring against yourself.
I'm all loose folds and ox-sized bones;

I was Giant Haystacks in the ring,
now I'm any man on the ropes.
Everyone's calling me by my given name.

The doctor talks of metastases
and morphine and the vanishing
tricks that malignant cells can play.

He'd put a fiver on me seeing in
the New Year with a stiff scotch
and a cigar, if he was a betting man.

November's almost here.

Ramblers

Awkward in their easy poses,
the snapshot leaves them walking wounded
through the day-released countryside.
John, falling behind, squints like an epidemiologist
into the microscope of the camera's lens.
He's always looking for microbes
on his red-raw hands.

Their distance and monolithic inwardness
are lies against what these ramblers once were:
men and women with young lives, talents
behind them, like villains in a pantomime;
the audience's shouts reminding them
of what they're missing. But they can't turn round.
They're left facing the camera on a field path in late spring;
heading home to their rituals, fending off the disorder
and the chaos they find behind everything.

Snowstorm Souvenir

It has the weight of that time
you pressed linen-fresh snow around a flint
to really dig at him.

Overwintering in Seville, your flamenco ended
with a bloody flourish and it snowballed from there:
the background poison-bottle blue,

filtering into the foreground of your lives.

Anatomy of a Liar

Slide beneath this infinite skin,
ride the network of my arteries,
travel the pathways of my sin.
I could tell you stories

about attraction, capillary and otherwise,
spin tall tales from the branches of my bronchioles,
take you to all four corners of my eyes.
I could design a thousand different roles,

palm you off with counting my goose pimples
to check that I am really still alive.
Perhaps I'll set you something simple,
as easy as letting out a lie.

Now, inching down from a hundred,
open me up like a rose. Reject
my heart and leave my lungs inflated,
they deceive you every time. Don't let

my tongue or throat divert you.
You'll have to cut me to the quick,
to my fingertips for a line that's true.
The rest's just a treat, a fleshed-out trick.

New York, Fourth of July

The yellow cabs in your black neighborhood
streak by like mustard on a hot dog,
full of the juice of gasoline. You climb the stairs
and the thirty-fifth floor of your high-rise
with its elevator laid low is,
for one night only, the best place to be.
The sky's gunpowder-plotted astrological chart
has your stars in the ascendant, going off
with paparazzi flashes of promise.
The Chrysler building, its lights like spilt milk,
blasts upwards over Midtown, failing to launch:
a rocket with its touch-paper keystone
held for a moment, then another and another,
by the car lights along 43rd and Lex.

The cab driver's name is Monplaisir,
and you tip him five bucks for the pleasure
it gives you. A quarter to nine on the Fourth of July:
from Flushing Meadows to Bryant Park, from the East
to the Hudson rivers, fireworks flash against the canvas
of the dark, abstract expressions of something
just beyond your grasp. Well, reach up,
catch them as they fall. The crowd's roar drums
tinnitus in your ears. Lights fountain down,
the sieved rays of multicolored suns. Let them come.
Walk the sidewalks, be among people,
smell the cordite, sift the night for the one
who was sucked through the eye of a needle.
a hole in the sky, from your life. The light of your life.

Free Divers Off Sardinia

It begins with a breath, a bit like life.
The average man can hold this for two minutes,
maybe three; the best train to over five
or a blackout, bait the sharks or get eaten by them.
They plunge beneath the waves like litmus paper,
come up blue with the nitrogen bubbling in their blood.
Sixty metres is the deepest they're allowed to go: lungs
compressed to one-seventh of their natural size.

The divers are goggle-eyed, wasp-waisted
with the pressure that forces organs up into ribcages,
hearts in their mouths beating twenty per minute.
The slow blues. Some make the news dead or alive,
like the one who claimed his prize as he broke sixty metres
on his way down, trod water like a liquid astronaut
to break the surface on his way up, saying
Could've gone twice as deep, and split his sides.

Midnight in Midwinter
on Midsummer Common

for Charlotte

The fingers of the treetops
pull down the night sky like a blind.
Moths have eaten stars into its fabric;
it is an old world in which we live.

The town snaps itself out of its revelry
by midnight. The path home from here
will always lead to your street and your house,
wherever you are. This square half-mile

of green has tucked down under the cover
of night and the town is filled with the eye
of the moon. The common is a silver moon-dial
and I am the gnomon chasing my shadow

around the hours, clutching a trail
of mistletoe plucked from the winter
trees made bereft for you. I send you
a frosted kiss, a gift over the miles.

The Sower of Provence

He sowed seeds each day
with the patience
of a stone,
set ten thousand years
on waiting for a god
that never came.

Trees grew up where he had
struck through, planted
and patted down
and a forest came
to the place
which each man before
had declared barren
as a face in Hell.

He walked his woods
each day, this striker-through,
planter and patter,
and each day he thanked
a god that came perhaps
to him alone
for the blessing of patience
and green life.

The Cathedral Grimaces

The self-effacing gargoyles –
    ashamed of their own ugliness –
and those sticking their tongues out
    in defiance at the world,
have been sandblasted, carved
    and cajoled back to flawed perfection.

Some day, even the question
    of whether all this can really matter
will decay into stony silence,
    to be answered by a blank stare –
beauty and imperfection being
    as fleeting as dust devils in the eye of a storm.

ROS BARBER

Ros Barber was born in 1964 in Washington DC, but her family moved to Colchester one year later. She studied biology at university before taking a year off to concentrate on her writing. However, she gave up writing poetry for eight years in her twenties, only beginning again around 1997 following the breakup of her marriage. She now lives in Hove with her three sons and teaches creative writing at the University of Sussex. Her poetry has been commended three times in the National Poetry Competition, and she was awarded the title of Blue Nose Poet of the Year 2000.

Many of Ros Barber's poems isolate the unspoken, often dark passions lurking within the mundane or commonplace; the flavour might be described by a phrase from 'Eve's Hobby', "The scent of sex drifting across suburban gardens". Her poems can be peculiarly affecting, as in the bittersweet 'Well' and the chilling study of manipulation of power that is 'He'd Push My Hands Together'. A sporadic rhymer, she often uses blank or free verse; yet poems such as the Shakespearean sonnet 'Endnote' included in this selection demonstrate her ability to work within stricter forms.

Well

What I remember most was the white intensity
of your scream. We still tickled then, not too old
at seventeen. Your hair waved shamelessly;
elemental energy seeped through your skin as though
through fissures in a cooling mantle. You were
beyond belief, and words flooded my mouth
like grief as the drowning current of your laughter
swept me away. All this time I've missed you.

He works hard, you sigh, shaking your straight hair still.
Before your first child arrived, he'd capped the spring
and watched it dry. Marshy ground, he says, and a shrill
or social mother, are three of the most insidious things.
It's a family business now, he markets the water
while you man the phone and take orders. Your daughters'
chalky faces on the label make it sell and seem
like a litre of your purity for one pound nineteen.

You were my idol. On a field trip to Bradwell
all our kids ago, we catalogued crabs and seaweed
from the nuclear heated streams that fed the beach.
We wrestled in the rancid estuary mud: strange fish
mutated from mermaids hewn from women. Our
laughter shrieked curlews and oystercatchers into
the arms of Essex sky. You were stronger then
than even the tide flooding the scars of our footsteps.

Potato-printed crabs and starfish cover your kitchen,
limpet the fridge. Your elastic daughters are threading
shells of irridescent plastic into necklaces, itching
their eczema absently. Over the sink, a formal wedding
photograph parades you as you used to be. Leave him,
I want to say, as you flake your scalp and briefly scold
your dessicated children. Be wild, be fatal, be cold,
wash him away, I pray, under the hush of your breathing.

Pronoun

You never say her name; I never ask.
Pronouns walk us far

through the late night confessions,
next morning reassessments.

Her unsaid name blows about us
uncatchable as willowherb fluff

and as light
and as ready to seed;

and as sleeplessness
mottles the pigments

in my skin
her name spells itself in melanin:

a soft, emergent tattoo.
Once, before I started loving you,

I rang you at home.
A female voice on the answerphone

paired up your names like jacks,
like silver cruets,

like evening gloves,
smoothing them out at the elbows.

Hers was there, pressed against yours
and I thought of two corpses

discovered embracing
in the ruins of a fallen building,

having loved each other
to death.

Pearls

Lovers come in strings, they say, like pearls.
The glow of each belies a heart of grit
that itched the oyster's tenderness to fit
them up with nacre, near-identicals:
same feel, same form. Reflective flattery
that coats the neck in kisses; opens the mouth
to a careless, ragged hole. I wear them out,
rolling their surface lustre over me.
Yes, I am knotting lovers in a string –
the married men; the frail; the fractured youths –
and glossing them to smooth my suffering.
For emptiness must swallow awkward truths:
the oyster, entered, has no choice but groan
and form the lover's beauty from her own.

Old School Friends

Suddenly they gleed into her life,
clutching an insincerity of wishes,
condolence bundled up in bow and cellophane;
the sympathetic gabardine of every raincoat
puddling late November through her hall.

Like prows and bows and bells they came,
clanging their metalled hides against a grief
that had dropped out from the pockets of the sky,
a shot swan, an arrow of eye that had seen beyond
the glittering flattened fields of their insides.

There was an arrogance of time between them,
cushioned decades that they plumped and throned,
although for months before she'd sat alone,
blistering her throat with mute replies
as cancer slid its news beneath her door.

And then, one by one, they fetched their coats.
They made her up, and made themselves believe
their promises to write, or call. And took their keys.
And left their flowers to die before her eyes
as though they had not thought of her at all.

Endnote

I think of you as dead; it's easier
to live with you as some delinquent ghost
than live aware you love and live with her.
To keep this fiction true, I haunt the coast
with men who wear your clothes along the front
or feed the slots with coins that knew your hands
before I killed you off. They bear the brunt
of populating half-baked ampersands –
me & x. But when the plot runs out
there's only me & me & me & me:
poetic ego gorging on the doubt
with all the pointlessness of simile.
You live and breathe. And in the snooker halls
the boys rack up my grief like so much balls.

The Dancer

She could fold herself in a perfect half
like a dollar bill in a waitress's apron pocket,
waiting to be spent.

She could fold herself like an envelope,
the flat white surface of her thigh against
the flat white surface of her breastbone,
you could lick the edges of her together,
your saliva gumming her closed.

She could fold herself as flour
is folded into beaten eggwhite,
without knocking out the air.

And you would fold her back on herself
like the sleeve of an ironed shirt,
press her knee gently against her shoulder
before you entered – I know
this alien intimacy because once

you pressed my knee gently against my shoulder
before you entered, forgetting
that not all women are dancers.

Now you have returned to her suppleness
I am learning to fold in my own way,
like a bad hand in five card brag,
concealing my face, rubbing
the over-stretched elastic of my ligaments.

Eve's Hobby

Love's circumstantial scraps
blooming like funeral lilies on
my sheets began it: the avarice.

When I couldn't bear to wash free
his parting shot; when I couldn't
bring myself to purity, I fell to this.

Others collect mail-order figurines,
porcelain bears or reproduction
coins: untender things. But I

catalogue what others have
and I have not. The scent of sex
drifting across suburban gardens,

tangled in stunted fruit trees.
The elsewhere smile of the girl
waiting for a bus in flesh tone tights.

The couples half-having it through
clothes on the slopes of the park:
tendril limbs, tongues buried deep

in each other's mouths. And then there's
the matter of fact. Banana-coloured
condoms by the bandstand:

I pick them up when no one's looking.
Latex stretched to the shape of desire,
moulded by the cocks of strangers;

those prized, thickening globes
of semen, and the crusting juices
of women men entered but did not fill.

Summer finds me sprawled, awake,
across his ancient imprint, windows
gaping for new and precious

additions: the lilt of bedsprings
in the pilot's upstairs apartment,
the bruising chill of unexpected laughter.

He'd Push My Hands Together

to make me pray. His big hands; he had so much power
in his fingers and he'd squeeze like he could fuse the nubs
of my knuckles together if only God would give him
that extra p.s.i. The tendons rolled over each other

like garden canes in a gale and he wouldn't stop
until they crackled like the fireworks I could only ever
watch each year from my bedroom window. He said
Bonfire Night was heathen, like chocolate eggs,

carved pumpkins, Christmas trees; wouldn't have
such things in the house, and when he caught me
praying to the Easter bunny, he beat the skin off my thighs
with a four by two, and that's when I stopped praying.

God's love, he said, is a father's love, and both
he and God had to be harsh. Sometimes I couldn't
tell them apart. God the Father glared down invisibly
from the bathroom ceiling when I jerked myself off.

Father God glared at my unclasped hands from the pulpit
at Family Service and Evensong and I knew there'd be
hell to pay. At home, the comfort of instant retribution:
saying (or not saying) grace formed the holy trinity

of beatings: breakfast, lunch and tea. Morning prayer,
bedtime prayer; and at other times he'd vindictively
drop to his knees for no reason; I'd be doing my homework
or watching a wildlife documentary and he'd growl

Let Us Pray. But I was growing up and he was shrinking,
and my hands became his hands, and his diminished
until he hadn't the strength to fuse mine in supplication.
He called me from his bed and I made him wait, and wait,

almost drunk on the power. When he stopped calling
I went to him, his eyes glowing like the fragile bulbs
on a Christmas tree. *Pray for me*, he whispered,
and tapped his tiny hands against my palms.

Airtight

This was her breakfast this morning: coffee, toast
with thin-shred marmalade – lime – but just two bites
before scraping it into the bin. Later I'll touch
the craters her fingers left, the compressed crust
cut out by the mouth I'd die for. I'll memorize
the ragged half-moon of incisors that twist and jut

a little out of line. And then see if
that long-haired creep she kisses on the step
has had her yet. She must know he's not right
for her. A cheapening lout who makes me sift
through onion skins for evidence of his inept
attempts at 'love': the flabby Fetherlite.

There's nothing yet, thank God. But women are
a danger to themselves. She chats to guys
in Waitrose stacking shelves. Has no idea
the risks she takes each day: she's getting far
too friendly with the postman. That lamb-like smile.
But I'll protect her somehow. Keep her clear.

She's beginning to wreck my life. Even asleep
she ghosts her waking form across my screen:
rewind, replay and pause. Eating alone
or tripping across the lawn to hang out sheets
and smalls: the intimate loop of her routine
possesses me. She's thin now. White as bone.

She slept in her clothes last night. She's becoming a slut.
I've seen her weeping for hours into the phone
as though all that contrition could make her good
again. She's scared. She nailed her windows shut.
When the light goes off I'll call to let her know
I'm taking care of her. Well someone should.

KATHRYN GRAY

Kathryn Gray was born in Caerphilly in 1973 and
grew up in Swansea, going on to study German and
then Medieval Studies at the Universities of Bristol
and York. She spent a year teaching English in
Vienna. She began writing in 1998 and has received an
Eric Gregory Award in 2001. She currently lives in
North London and works as a civil servant.

Kathryn Gray looks likely to be one of the main
players in a resurgent group of young Welsh poets.
She began writing only three years ago and, like Greta
Stoddart, John Stammers, Julian Turner and Paul
Farley (a noticeable, but not intrusive influence on her
work), has thrived with the help of Michael
Donaghy's City University group. She uses long,
clause-packed lines to explore the lives of family and
friends in Swansea and London, then and now.

Aim

Your brother would bear down the barrel
of a shotgun intent on blasting our summers,
the force kicking back at his shoulder.
Through his mutters, he could hear it
in the tall grasses and displaced earth
ahead and toward him. For years, the false aim
that went clean through his trainer,
left one toe lopped, was his proof there was life
in those fields. Thinking of him then –
those affected sniper eyes, that hobbled foot,
thumb and finger inched this close to a catch,
how he fell at a single report, was found
one noon by children – how could we have known
that in there, breathing, under those long days,
he'd met himself coming the other way.

Sign

Inasmuch as our intentions are what we leave behind
in error and return for later, here is the empty leather
of a wallet, the mobile, cigarettes, a lighter
and in certain weather, the scarf and black umbrella;
ring removed, its emphasis tinkle in my water glass . . .

And you are at my door in the morning, to reclaim it all
to trouser and breast pocket; cashmere around your neck,
hair run through and the quickest of glances in the mirror.
The scissors of two fingers snap at the bubbles,
the gold chink as you fish it out. In your other hand,
limp wings hang from broken spokes. I dry coffee cups,
string their handles on the rack. One of these days,
I tell them, you will stay the night. And then I take that back.

Friend,

when we find ourselves once more on the floor
of Indian restaurant, public house or pushed back
to cigarette-scarred polyprop seats of taxi rank,
loud and right for the drink we've sunk,
each wrestled down to her quick for past wrongs:
the birthday missed, the boyfriend shared,
skirt returned, but torn, never to be worn again . . .

when they pull us apart and threaten the police
and we walk out to a pavement loose with rain,
slivers of kebab meat and our bared toes brace
against the stipples that come heavier, and we are
not together, one a yard ahead of the other, arms
crossed, miles from morning doorsteps, two women
on an A-road and we stop to explain to one another . . .

please be quiet, come nearer and let our cupped hands
pool the languages of loose change, mascara, fiver.

Ceremonies

We always have the ubiquitous sandwiches to rely on,
the modest spread at the strapped reception or anniversary,
or around such youwill find the moribund parishioner
at the christening, who no one's ever met, slicking out
the unwieldy mess of cucumber and mayonnaise,
who finishes the lot, realigns her dentures, curses, passes on.
There is proof that you are not alone, if any were needed,
in the pyramid stacked over an almost Venetian doily
at the training weekend buffet or the pork luncheon staple
of the bingo halls, the potted crab you get at the lesser casinos,
their crusts fragrant with lager and lime. How each recalls
the delicate flourish that could only be your mother's
and your protests as she stacked them, wrapped around
the clingfilm or aluminium lovingly as swaddle.
And yet they remain unique as the smells of different houses:
the slightest variation in geometry, texture and filling once
held up after school against the off-white of a glass of milk
in a house that was not your own, where you detected
foreign fingerprints that revolted, sunk, wet in the middle
of the thin-sliced Sunblest.

                    Now, with the spring of the hinge,
shop-bought, I may find a stray hair, the lacquered shave
of a nail, cuticle from some girl down on the production line,
petrified between the butter and lettuce and take it vaguely
as a comfort on this bench, intoxicated by its significance.
I chew through rye and find endless doorsteps, cold chicken
abandoned at the back of a fridge, our entire history of bread
that even if written would remain unread and I meditate
the women in black lined up at the Formica after the service,
who remind me, choked to a whisper, that my job it is (hand
gently guided), to dip into the softness of grated cheese
in the Pyrex bowl I can hardly reach, make a fist, scatter.

Gideon

Little I take from our weekends away,
Mostly minutiae: tablets of soap, pink
As babies, pressed floral tissues and shrink
Back of serrated-edged shampoo sachets.
But then, these are how I mark our days
Apart, when, in need of the slightest link,
I open the bathroom cabinet, and think
How it happens: hotels, afternoons laid
Down, distant couplings of bedside tables
Like marriages; those hidden Visa slips
At the bottom of my underwear drawer –
Bra straps over months of signature;
Nights, acts of faith, when I bend the lamp, dip
Its neck, my hands smooth over a bible.

Driver

Where exactly on this road it was they dipped
their heads, got in and were driven away
to be back in bed – as they'd said – by eleven,
no witness could remember or agree, but as we go
along at about 70, and you turn the radio up

I start to think of their laughter, their arms held out,
thumbs straining at the cars that passed them,
the way they might have pushed each other,
swayed, and then a Ford slowed, his face lowered,
he leaned over as the nearside window wound down.

One goes in the front and turns to her friend
again and again, and it could be any other night.
Knitted sleeves rub on the brown leatherette.
Here and there a stray fibre falls. He says nothing,
turns off just before the lights to Jersey Marine.

It is already behind us in the rear-view mirror.
And when we stop, the two of us slam the doors,
watch the boot of your car go around the corner,
it's then things occur: the coiled length of washing
line I saw, a blue sweater I left on the back seat.

The Book of Numbers

The last four digits of your number I can't remember:
the first might be her winning call at bingo,
some of the houses (evens on a street) I never lived in.
A pack of John Player's, then double Mahler's
whatever, the Chanel counter, acrylic sienna daubed
into an earlobe-shaped space on the canvas
or a coin produced from a sleeve, during an evening's
prestidigitation and the deck of incontinent cards
that spills and skims from the croupier's hands.
The times shuffle for each departure gate at Heathrow
or the trains on a station concourse I've memorized
in no particular order, a date for Waterloo, then the buses
tour Trafalgar Square, the total degrees to all those angles,
collapsed roughly to the Equator, tiers becoming slices
of wedding cake; the vital per cent off that dress,
without which no man can buy or sell, or else a tetragram,
which brings me back more or less to what I mean,
the last four digits of your number I can't remember.

A Voyeur's Volume

A jaundiced Harold Robbins or Jackie Collins
you might hold on a balcony, the remnants
of previous occupants, like us, on the two-week,
no-see package; the way you might pronounce
svelte, draw it out to the tip of your tongue,
to where your foot might then reach along,
lift up my sarong, and it is quiet in the passage
of villas that runs on down below us. *Thigh*,
you say, your leg drawn back, and turn
to another page that has marked its line at the spine,
smiling to yourself and no one in particular.

The Italians in the Rain

You could almost see them down the backstreets
as it bucketed on a Saturday night, the purr
of a Vespa, his right foot pressed on the kerb
as he leans over, calls to a girl and she parleys
a while, then hops on, wraps herself around him.
Or along the sea front, in the mirrors of Sidoli's,
where a couple share a Neopolitan with one spoon,
the crest of biscuit between them, fight out
who gets the strawberry and who the chocolate.
You think it's just possible that she always knew
what he'd done with her best friend and sister.
Quicker than the grabbed coat and clipped heels,
from Landore to Y Crwys, now you hear
the parked Fiats as they creak at the beauty spots,
slapped faces and the smashed bottles outside the bars.
And maybe you see there is a man who lifts up
the fryer with its welded batter or does the books
on a stool by the till, the packets of coffee on the shelves
behind him. There's a watercolour of St. Mark's
or the Trevi Fountain under the arrow to the toilets
and, as this rain shows no sign of stopping, he looks on
it all, gestures at two passers-by who try the door
a WE ARE CLOSED, returns to his work, forgets where he is.

Projectiles

On the other side of my ceiling, they're at it again,
and in your absence I have to piece together alone
the object as wedding gift, thrown or tipped.
Here, the lamp, its bulb dislocated or smashed.
There, dishes spin the length of the fitted kitchen.
Exchanges slip through the cavities, across
bathroom, bedroom, to be belted out in the hall.

And I want them to go on but only an hour passes
until they curl up against the pillows, fists relax
on the sheets. This early light splits through
a bottle of perfume, the dust is a kind of sickness.
Next door's baby screams the morning imperatives.
Your letters still arrive at this address: each one tilts,
nosedives from the brush of a shared letterbox.

Alibi

This is what I knew of him: a glass of Dark
held against the mahogany bar, while public parks,
the broad and even lawns of crematoria
thickened at noon; the garden hut's door
which stood ajar (in front, a green deckchair
stretched out and full of sun); a verso stare
in an optic-lined mirror; the benefits
of geranium explicated through the hiss
of my Bitter pulled and frothed to the brim;
that all those years the council never sacked him.
His art was to be in the two places at once.
Back then, for those summer months,
I listened harder than I'd ever done
to good advice *Make it look like you'll come*
around the corner any second, everything
casual, like . . . I always leave a bit of something
behind. Yes, those lost days crowd into nights
now, when I think of the slump and rise of lights
on the fruit machine, its spiral turn
which seemed interminable, or the quick burn
as a torn-off green swatch of betting slips
in the ashtray caught at an Embassy Filter Tip.
I wonder is it best mid-April or early May
to plant, what (between gulp and drag) he'd say.
Or if this is what I can't or won't see
as I knock my last spare change at an empty
bar: how the grass, on a day like today, will grow,
in a town like the one outside, and know
it's no longer a matter of being here or there
and that, for once, he is not elsewhere.

SIÂN HUGHES

Siân Hughes was born in 1965 in Potter's Bar and grew up in a small village in south Cheshire. Her jobs have included teaching infants and community publishing with Somali families in Moss Side; she was Education Officer at The Poetry Society and now writes for educational publications. Her first poems appeared in 1996, when 'Secret Lives' won the Times Literary Supplement/Poems On the Underground Competition. Smith/Doorstop published a pamphlet, *Saltpetre,* in 1998, and Southern Arts gave a writer's award in 2000.

Siân Hughes writes poems characterized by a tautness and economy that can initially give a deceptive impression of simplicity. Indeed, those which are superficially lightest – such as the delightful 'Chaucer' or the comic vignettes 'Taxi' and 'The Girl Upstairs' – are often the ones which offer more with each successive reading. The principle of economy applies also to her less humorous poems: see, for example, the enigmatic 'The Sacking Offence', which achieves its aims by suggesting rather than stating.

Romance

The Crammond children had a talent for romance,
the grand gesture. Dying was their special field –
no one outside the family could match them for panache.
Uncle David died of opera: a long queue in the rain
set him coughing in act three. Despite vigorous swigs
from his hip-flask, he was home before the fifth.

Love of engines did the trick for Archie,
just back from the war, too weak
to survive hand-cranking his pet Austin.
Travel took Herbert, the damp air, the women,
though to his credit he reached Constantinople
ahead of the plague and died at the card table.

Janet lasted long enough to have two girls
before the New World took their father
and her will to live. Which left Polly
to button her nieces into good winter coats
and threaten 'you'll catch your death',
as if he might join them in a game of kiss-chase.

Rabbit Skin

The winter their mother went into the ground
it had to be split with a pick. Without her
they forgot how to keep themselves warm,

stood still too long, stopped playing pat-a-cake
out in the courtyard, 'clap hands, clap hands,
till Daddy comes home'. They knew he wouldn't.

When Grandfather Crammond lifted the doe
clear of the hutch, knocked her cold with a cobble stone
and turned her inside out, they learned

the cost of two pairs of rabbit skin gloves,
that animals have chilblains under their fur,
that red is an acceptable colour for eyes.

Taxi

In the taxi you say 'I know this part of town.
Or I used to, years ago, when I had a tart.

That is the right word for it, isn't it: "tart"?'
'Not really,' I say, and unbutton my coat.

'She had a terrible yappy dog, but I didn't care.
She was nice and fat. I liked that. Fat.'

I lift my dress over the tops of my stockings.
'Fat' you say again, 'lovely and fat.'

Fidelity

According to the magazine I picked up at the airport
that caramel-brown mongrel who followed you the length of the
    beach
is the lucky colour for your star sign, one you should wear every
    day.
He suited you, it's true, his long snout lifted to your waist
as he kept perfect time with your feet, pointer-fashion.
In the evening light the high-stepping ripples of his shadow
as it crossed the tide-marked sand suggested something pedigree.

Today I saw him tack out from behind the windsurf place
and slip into a pack of Germans on their way to the port, his
    smooth coat
an effortless match for their close-cropped heads and tans.
Long before they loaded the last rucksack onto the pilot boat
he was shedding gold flecks of blond light from his fur,
ducking into the shade behind a stack of blue plastic crates,
his eye on the slow swinging gait of a passing American.

Soap

The boy's face is his father's first stroke of luck –
before the child can lift his head from the blanket
wool manufacturers compete for the negatives.

It makes his Daddy's day to see him sit up and smile:
'Freddy, show your dimples to the nice gentleman,
I'm through at the elbows.' Nothing pays like soap.

Ten foot high, dressed in bubbles, he spends the winter
riding the sides of trolley buses up to Princess Street.
It's enough to make his sisters get down and walk.

Blanco pays the doctor's bills, Sudso goes on drink,
Pears pays for one and one-in-arms to America
where the boy can cut his teeth in style, on steak.

The Sacking Offence

Like the outline of a paperclip
left on the window-sill two summers ago,
or fingerprints, dusted over but still intact
along the edge of the franking desk,
something like cigarette smoke
might, even this far into the week,
uncurl from the corner of a desk,
to print last Friday, 10 p.m.,
as a row of inverted chimneys
across the calendar on the back wall.

Saltpetre

You taught me how to roll cigarettes
without saltpetre; the slightest draft blows them out.

I count your visitors in empty bottles, a steady drip
of something collecting under your chair.

There are slates in the guttering, dead leaves
and newspapers behind the door.

I'm preoccupied with the state of your collars
worn through to the webbing, lost buttons,

the damp under the windows, the problem of storage,
the way your shoe heels wear down on the diagonal,

a shadow that falls across your eyes
as if you were watching me undress.

The Double

Arsenal v. Newcastle. You stayed out of town
while I followed a small ad to a 'houseboat for one'
moored within earshot of the tropical aviary
where, having no engine, it had been for some time.
At the end of a line of painted narrow boats
the one I could afford was peeling black plastic
over a mottled hull, no pots of nasturtiums,
no friendly dog, no crate of lager over the side.

The windows had been sealed in the winter
with insulation tape, and never reopened.
The toilet arrangement was a bucket and hose
and relied on the cover of darkness. This was June,
but I made light of the way the midday sun
turned the boat into a man-sized methane tank.
The owner brushed a gas-ring with his cigarette
to demonstrate the heating – high or low.

I was home before the whistle, but all the way
from Holloway Road, the Piccadilly Line
was full of shouting, singing and red scarves.
Well beyond the last time you might have phoned
the windows rattled in time to a slow drive-past
with horn-blowing and sirens. At the end of a season
of hard knocks and missed opportunities, one side
takes to the streets to celebrate the double.

The Girl Upstairs

The girl upstairs wears white lycra shorts
even in winter. 'They're comfy'
she says. 'What's the problem?'
From the half landing you can hear
the steady scratch of her electric meter.

The corner shop sends messenger boys
up the road with her grocery boxes.
Cling peaches in syrup. Carnation milk.
Baby carrots. Peas. Her freckles
are pale orange under a home made tan.

The landlord says 'She could make it nice,
homely, but she's not the type.'
Her boyfriend laughs. 'When I come home
I don't want gardening and all that crap.
Fornication. That's what a man needs.'

Chaucer

Chaucer was adept at shortcrust pastry –
he discovered it needn't be used as a pot lid
and cast aside when the meat was cooked,
but added wild herbs, rocket, best butter,
kept it cool in an earthen pot in a stream
and rolled it out perfectly smooth.

That joke about the Friar's blancmange
was a serious matter – he'd spent years
perfecting something like Angel Delight
for which he ground lump sugar very fine.
It's said the muscles of his egg-whisk arm
were rock solid, and very few knew why.

Secret Lives

Sometimes your dressing gown unhooks
And slides out under the garden door,
With three aces up his sleeve.

He flies in the face of next door's dog,
Backflips down the middle of the street,
Opening himself to the breeze.

Something in pink nylon flutters a cuff
From an upstairs window. He twirls his cord
To beckon her outside.

They're heading for a club they know
Where the dress code is relaxed midweek,
And the music is strictly soul.

Map-Reading

All our wrong turnings bring us
Through the same Sunday village,
Past the same couple, watching
From deckchairs in their garden –

Against the holiday traffic,
Down a one in four we had to get out
And look at for a while, to believe
We could tip ourselves into it and live –

Back to a set of traffic lights
Outside a bingo hall in Potter's Bar
Where I refold the map the wrong way
And throw it onto the back seat.

A.B. JACKSON

Born in Glasgow in 1965, Andrew Buchanan Jackson was raised in the town of Bramhall, Cheshire, later receiving his secondary education at Bell Baxter High School in Cupar, Fife. After abandoning the idea of going to Art School, he studied English Literature at Edinburgh University and went on to work in cinemas and pubs in Edinburgh, Dublin and Glasgow. In 2000 he completed a postgraduate MSc degree, and now works at the Glasgow College of Building and Printing.

A.B. Jackson has two predominant styles. The first is a lyrical, observational poetry based in urban, night-time settings: his poems often seem to be about those things glimpsed creeping or shining in the darkness. The other is a denser, blank verse in a higher style and on a grander scale which he uses to explore psychological and religious ideas. He is also a talented artist and musician, and these qualities are apparent in his delicate, musical language.

Rewind: 1965

The egg ferments, the one cell splits in two:
again, four: again, eight: sixteen: thirty-two.
Droplets of fat, like miniature dabs of butter,
nourish and sustain. Welcome, morula,
little mulberry . . . free-falling, spineless,
until, upon the uterine surface,

touchdown. Transparent, semi-opaque, solid,
the heart comes to fruition, big as a head.
Welcome, tiddler, mild water-scorpion.
Gills disappear, cartilage becomes bone.

Full term: seismic waves, electrical storms,
the twelve-hour haul of not being born,
between two worlds – induced. I make it late,
my first descent of many to the light.

A Ring

1

You and I could be, knowing just this much –

in times of flood, clamber to the roof;
wear day-glo orange, holler. Train your sight
on tiny omens. Take them as a truth.

On orchard walls, new buds and barbed wire.
In the cat's jaws, game, as we're in love.

2

The kitchen table, the bed where we move
to serve ourselves the long meal of a kiss –

the lost and found debris of togetherness:
wine bottles, underwear, dead birds, amethyst –

the granny wallpaper: identical ships
on their small identical pedestals of sea.

3

With both of us asleep, the room wakes up,
a durable masque of curtains, ashtrays, cups.
They see what lies between us, face to face:

an hourglass – a space dividing proles.

Let's taunt our eyes eternally with this,
let's always cancel one or other out.

4

Fuzzy, undefined, we look again –

our city stands, a forest of alarms,
TV aerials, dogs chewing footballs;
a broken sign which reads: *Salvation Arm.*

Invisible, the rainbow's other half,
the sister-arc that ploughs beneath the earth.

The Christmas Pet

A blood-sport refugee
kicking its heels in sanctuary.
It was an impulse buy,

spurred on by the children
and the straw season.
Care required, minimum:

recommended food, anything,
make the den inviting,
give the gold nose-ring

a good polish.
It did not flourish;
I offered barley and mash

without success. It grew
lean and repetitive, slow,
lean and repetitive. Now,

having churned up the lawn,
it patrols
the small circle of indoors

scoring things with precise horns.

Stammer

Dear larynx, Venus
fly-trap of a throat,
just spit it out –

frogs, hiccups,
the words
'Innocence' and 'Icarus'.

Telephones are dangerous.
I come across
like a howler-monkey,

vocalizing high
in the green canopy.
How exotic!

It's ridiculous.
My first name stalls
at 'A——,' a dumb horse.

So who, to wit, who?
Dear Coherence,
thank you, goodbye, thank you.

In Memory of R.D. Laing

1927–1989

The end: a simple matter. St Tropez,
cardiac arrest while playing tennis.
Our death is different, mobile, compatible
with breathing, making love or tea or money.

Two-bit dramas in ruined amphitheatres;
a sense of loss provoked by life this time.
Not to be undone, we, in our static
paradise of todays, whitewash our recent

pasts with our recent wallpaper, reduce
your passion to a comfortable cliché –
The insane are sane and vice versa?
Obvious trash. This was not your message.

You saw a man whose muscles turned to bone.
For the age, an image; petrified mass
from which the eyes stared out. With inner ground
so profitably set aside, we work,

and every hour divine some higher purchase.
So who or what to blame? Genealogist
of pain, you hauled the Family up for trial;
you, a Protestant Scot, religion sprung

from Calvin, Luther, constipation's martyrs,
a nation stripped of saints and given *Discipline*.
Of course we weep as European walls
are broken. How could we dance? There's freedom

and there's freedom. Ours is a well-stocked fridge;
the human psyche quartered like a pie
in self-healing binges; a middle class occult.
One by one we have hijacked ourselves.

Demands? Just this: that the long not feeling
at home should end. Distance. Unbalance.
No wonder: we've placed so much faith in the air
and the air is so silent now we're so well

and truly in it, taking brief snapshots
of Earth from orbit. Earth so far from touch,
a world below that grows to nought, as systems
fail their checks, and links are lost, and we find Space.

Goodbye body. The mind's out on a limb.
What else could we do but close ranks among
mutual conspiracies of the heart,
we, the half-baked, eternal unmarried,

salvation or nemesis lying wholly
with dear ones loved to death? *Create*, you said.
And here was cause for praise: Art's descent,
unearthing the heart's apocryphal text

in Christ's long shadow, growing darker still
against our legislation of the light.
We cast our own divisions in the sun,
before, behind, within, each way we turn.

Your arrival, timed to imperfection,
was rude but not uncalled for: at best,
new sense was made: an unconditional chance
to be misunderstood beyond all guilt.

Hopefully we can return the favour,
forgive you for taking refuge in booze:
you did what any decent madman would,
being torn by factions, furious with God.

You wanted Him, more than most, argued
for angels in Glasgow, London, Iona.
The truth is you ran with us all, but looked back.
And we froze

Journey

The early nutter had caught his worm:
me, worn ragged with Guinness, 3 a.m.
on the last bus reserved for the head-broken.

His voices railed in concert, a paragon
of nonsense. *Duck soup! British Home Stores!* On
and on. I wished him grievous bodily harm,

all sympathy with my bearings gone
until – looking out – *there* was Orion,
disabled into stars, who was born a man . . .

I carried him with me as an arrow,
back through time, up forty miles of road,
his belt a notch off-kilter. The moon followed;

I thought of Jean-Dominique Bauby on his pillow,
paralysed except for one eyelid, slowly
winking his way towards *Fin*, his limbs in tow.

And with some bitterness I thought of you,
half-cut, dishing up your favourite quote:
A memory of love, a green meadow.

Corners came, gears moved down. By 4 a.m.
I stood in the bright vacant heart of Glasgow.

Missing

Tell me of the scattering of the man who is saved: who are mixed with him, and who are divided from him?

ZOSTRIANOS, 45.4–5

He wanders lost in a blue
   green T-shirt and bedroom slippers
   guided by the patron saint of travellers
His printed face joins the queue at bus shelters
Seven miles from his mantelpiece he beds down
His solar-powered watch is faithful to the time
He sleeps with his head in Spain
   and his feet in Springburn
Mercury turns retrograde to Mars
At midnight he enters a market garden
   where, as prophesied, he eats
   tomatoes and strawberries
At 4 a.m. he is courted by the rain
By 6 he is pronounced in love

The Temptation of Saint Anthony

And this thing dare I soothly say:
If that he were God veray,
Hunger shold greeve hym by no way;
That were against reason.

CHESTER 12: Butchers

I

Fire came down. A snap. A click.
The opening and shutting of a beak.

Lightning fertilized the ground –
and so, baptized, I quit the world
to fathom God: a wilderness
lay waiting to admit my flesh.

I saw the desert scorpion, black,
fully armoured, dusting up sand
as it scuttled from under a stone, sting
erect and itching for small prey.

Whatever I turned my mind to, hatched.
For six days I fed upon the sky.

2

There is a natural surrender:
knives in a glass of clear water,

all broken by light, yet still whole.
In God's grace I break my will.
And there, upon a groaning table,
animal breeds animal

eats animal, in bloody shifts –
wolves, livestock, flycatchers, flies,
the endless mauled sacrifice.
Creator Spiritus, what *is* this.

I make a circle here, and sit.
On brutal earth, on earth as it is –

3

The sun works on my mouth.
In prayer, words turn and taste sour.

All sense has fallen to one fact:
circulating in the bloodstream's net
a splinter of the Cross, its course
fixed blind upon my central heart.

Fever holds me high in its wings.
You my companion, architect of shadows,
tell me what appetite will serve. I know.
Your eyes are a hornets' nest of light.

The sun shakes its yellow rings.
A thorn tree buds with gold coins.

4

The stars' mill-wheel shone.
Without warning this clear vision –

A ploughed moonlit field, a man
by jackals torn   to radiance

Bone-meal, grist, immortal soul
all fuel the furnace of the Cross

*

The desert dimmed. Rocks gave way
to gathering voices I knew and loved;
at one, delivered back to the world,
I found it very much the same.

I know the cities and their names.
A host of horn-billed angels sing.

Filing

Oncology Centre. Cast–iron cabinets
of case histories, fresh figures, a request
in triplicate for a 'marrow harvest'...
I picture a bumpkin surgeon, in a sweat,
sorting cells like apples into buckets.

Facts are sensitive here. I work my way
through bales of personal files (always 'cancer'),
my throat cracked by so much dusty paper.
Truth comes to light on X-ray:

someone's brain, a wrinkled slice of fruit;
the skull's bone, a phosphorescent hoop,
classified and coded. Someone who.

Dear X, whatever daily face you wear,
may you never falter, never flower.

TABISH KHAIR

Tabish Khair is an assistant professor in the Department of English, Copenhagen University. Born in 1966, in Ranchi, India, he has an M.A. from Magadh University in his home town of Gaya (India), a Ph.D. from Copenhagen University and has previously worked as a journalist for *Times of India* (Delhi) and *Politiken* (Copenhagen). *Babu Fictions*, his study of contemporary Indian English fiction was recently published by Oxford University Press. He is also the author of a novel and four collections of poems. He won the All India Poetry Competition in 1995–96.

Already one of India's most successful younger poets, Tabish Khair's work will be new to most British readers; for this reason we have included him in this anthology as an exception to the series rule of introducing poets yet to publish a collection. He is a poet of memory, family matters and landscape, cataloguing the sights and scents, customs and weather of both his native country and his current adopted one. In a poem such as 'Kites of Another Kind', he shows a typical, deft balance of sentiment and detail to evoke the changing nature of Indian childhood.

Nurse's Tales, Retold

Because the east wind bears the semen smell of rain,
A warm smell like that of shawls worn by young women
Over a long journey of sea, plain and mountains,
The peacock spreads the Japanese fan of its tail and dances,
And dances until it catches sight of its scaled and ugly feet.

Because the *koel* cannot raise its own chicks –
Nature's fickle mother who leaves her children on doorsteps
In the thick of nights, wrapped in controversy and storm –
Because the *koel* will remain eternally young, untied,
It fills the long and empty afternoons with sad and sweet
    songs.

Because the rare *Surkhaab* loves but once, marries for life,
The survivor circles the spot of its partner's death uttering
    cries,
Until, shot by kind hunters or emaciated by hunger and loss,
It falls to the ground, moulting feathers, searching for death.
O child, my nurse had said, may you never see a *Surkhaab* die.

Mango Recipes

That summer the storm was a lightning raid.
Water gurgled down pipes, splurged
From corners and crevices. Hail exploded
Into spray splinters on the driveway. We watched

Your tender, tended rosebushes shudder
From the machine gun impact of fat
Raindrops, counted the unripe mangoes
Being rifled by the wind, wondered

If any fruit would survive the storm, watched
The toddy trees bending over like
Shelled soldiers, counted the ways
One could prepare unripe mangoes:

Tarkari, pickle, chutney... wondered why
You had not called. When the telephone rang,
My aunt heard the thunder, feared to pick it up.
When she did suddenly all sounds ceased.

Arm

The lifting of the arm is an art. You
Did it with the grace of a queen. Here
The sight of an arm lifting
To ward dust or hair from eye brings to mind
The absence of bangles. In this land
Of bare arms, I bare my memories of you
Parsimoniously.

Loss is a way of life once
You start packing memories in suitcases:
I will not break the glass of my memory
Of your lifted arm brushing away dust
Or hair. Your fingers were kneaded with flour.
Sunlight caught in your bangles.

If I were to tell them this, they
Will want to know why you wore bangles.
Was it steel, they will ask, or was it glass. How
Can you make such thin bangles of glass? What
If a woman refuses to wear bangles in India?

If I were to tell them about the lost art
Of lifting a bangled arm to brush back hair,
They will turn to me and ask – smiling
Like my Danish friend four months ago –
You took her to bed then?

Distances

A paper rustle from the needle highway
Makes him look down through the trees, startled
By distance. This is the farthest he has been
From the hours that are filed on his office desk.

Here days can be scratched on stone, etched
On wet bark. There is no trace of the small hours.
Another language is heard. A different colour.
But what he marks most is a quality of distance

That can change roaring metal contraptions to paper
And hone down broad busy highways to needles
Of bone. He has practised distances all his life,
But they have been measured like beads on a thread

Or those words of polite dismissal over porcelain
With which one can lose a friend or a past with the ease
Of pouring tea. Such implacability of distance
Disturbs him. He sees the trees, tall and separate.

No Theorems

No theorems in the Khair family equation,
You once said when we were computing
The angle our town made with your dreams.

What you had in mind were family bickerings,
The usual inventory of who said what and to whom
That we later bind into albums of memories.

But today when the sun has lightened this foreign day
And the leaves of a nameless tree in this backyard
Are shoals of herring following the current of the wind

Which smells of sea, it always does here, the wind
That is so different from the earthy wind of our town
And childhood, a wind that had left sea 500 miles ago

And was shouldering on with the mature burden of water
To the impossible dream of snow-clad peaks. Or was dry
And taciturn with age, loss, bitterness.

The lines I have written before will not do for you
Or the land you never forsook and that holds you,
The lines I have written bear too much of a place

Where sea is separated from land by a simple line.
Where I come from, where you are there lies more
Between sea and earth than men write of, and heaven

Is another matter. No theorems then, as you said,
In the Khair family equation, just the unmeasured
Other geometries of who said what and to whom.

The Maidservant, Now Married

Our fourteen knotted years would have kneaded me,
Learning the flinty alphabets which could not be used
Except to chip the sounds that slipped from my lips
Into a glazed language mirroring you, inverted.

The cocoon of your ways, your cultivated softness
Would have turned me silk; but my flesh was hardened,
My skin callused doing what needed to be done
To keep your rooms in order, your hair in place.

Not your indulgence, not the thoughts you fed me like food,
Not the brittle gifts you clad me in like the bride's ephemeral
Garments, which I put on and off one harsh night of return,
I thank you for the tone of your voice that taught me to jump.

South Delhi Murder

For three days she took it for spilled red ink
Or nail polish. Then a scab of flies
Peeled to hint at the wounds shut
Behind that door. Her head buzzed
As she called the police. Such a sweet boy,
She later gasped to Mrs Guha, a little dense
But smiling and so-sweet, to think he bottled up
In himself the rage of 26 stabs, twen-tee-six,
You never can tell with these people, no, not ever.
To which Mrs Guha sadly shook her gold earrings.

The officer who turned up with two policemen
Also shook his head when told of the old couple
Who had lived in that flat with one serving boy
And presents from guilt-stricken sons in the US.
Having broken the door and located the crime,
He came out holding a large hanky to his nose,
Spat and asked, Nepali boy, no? Bihari *chokkra*?
Some clues are so obvious they don't have to be pinned:
The incision of murder is always the outsider's choice,
Someone on the edge of life, driven by ghostly scalpels.

Sometime in the morphia of night when the roads of Delhi
Were white swathes of loneliness and smog, sometime
Three or more nights ago when the occasional truck's
Back lights faded to wavering bandages of yellow,
Sometime in a gauzed silence broken by yapping
Street dogs, so-sweet Shyam had crept to the locked
Front door and let his accomplices in. Steel rods
Had been used, and knives; the old man clubbed in bed,
His wife surgically stabbed later. A cousin was asked
By the officer to make an inventory of missing items.

Which was long: two TV sets, radio, Banarasi *saris*
All the inherited silver, jewellery, cash, in fact everything
Of value except the laptop, which had been left behind

In panic or ignorance of its value. Bihari *chokkras*,
Scoffed the officer, what do they know of computers,
Or alphabets for that matter. It turned out that this time
The *chokkra* in question had been filmed, holding
Loaded trays in parties, and his address noted.
Justice was clinical, sweet Shyam nabbed in his village
With fifty rupees on him and a *sari* for his mother.

Almost a Ghazal for my Grandfather's Garden

A flock of sparrows leaves the *mehndi* bush like a shudder.
Two squirrels chase each other around the trunk of a *kathal*.

Herons stand stilted like village ancients beside the pool.
The soft coo of a pigeon betrays neither distance nor place.

Parrots squabble on the bare top branch of the spreading
　　gullar.
Five orange trees hunch laden with unplucked and acrid
　　fruit.

The pomegranate plant still retains a cracked, crowned *anár*.
Mango trees stand mute, lacking their summer voices of
　　yellow.

The ladybird changes from spotted red to a whirr of wings.
Half-plates of dark mushroom jut from the fallen log.

Grass is an intricate network of roads travelled by black ants.
The earth below is a breathing skin, veined with dark roots.

A dry green shell is all that is left of the snail and his tracks.
Translucent wings are all that will remain of dragonflies.

Perhaps I should put my faith in the crow and the
　　subversive rat.
A bunch of builders measure out lines and angles from
　　a blueprint.

Kites of Another Kind

Our kites were flimsy. They were not hoiked
To pierce a foreign heaven; they rode the slender
Currents of air, their sharpened strings sagging
Under the weight of a palpable sky which suddenly
Squalled and tugged and pulled in our arms like a baby.

There was an art to flying, but the sharpening of strings
Was a science. You needed finely ground glass, glue
Made from flour, egg yolk and rice-water: all of which
Had to be applied in the right proportion and the string
Suspended between pegs from roof to ground to dry.

Roofs were the runaway of our flights, the cockpit
From which we monitored our dogfights of paper
And tight skeletons of wood. Danger lurked
In the corner of the eye with no computerized beep
Of warning, and sometimes trees jumped at our kites.

                    *   *   *

All this, of course, is Sanskrit to the small boy
You have shanghaied to the bare, memory-littered roof
Of your parents' partly locked house. He has a new
And colourful computer game waiting for him below;
His skies are different and farther away than yours.

He looks around in bored incomprehension and, suddenly,
You see the nakedness of skies. Where, his eyes ask,
Are the mythical cursors, the dots, dashes and demons,
Of your computer screen? There are no kites – though
It is winter, a time of gentle breeze and blue sky

When boys would man the control panels of your roofs,
Lever their light dreams of paper and sharpened string
Through a sky that was for four months accessible
And to hand. All the roofs stand mildewed and sullen.
Distant hilltops are haloed by kites of another kind.

Milk

Now it has reached this town of slow watches,
The sign that we are the world's largest producer of milk,
A proof in waterproof packets marked Mother Dairy.

It is one of the scripts of change, good, bad or illegible,
That this town offers to the wandering eye wondering
Why four years abroad have changed so much, and nothing.

This new three-wheeled van, loud and brash descendant
Of the stiff-jointed, slow-speaking Hero cycle poised
Between two unmarked cans, equal on both sides.

Though even this van does not seem to have stopped some,
Like my father, from having their milk brought to them on four
Legs, and a man wearing a loose turban and a moustache

Who takes the pail set out for this purpose and holding
It firm between feet moves his hands in an ancient rhythm,
Filling the morning with the magic sound of monsoon.

1.15 A.M.

Below the highway darkness turns the heath
To ancient shapes, to where the wind is hooves,
The mist a cloak swirling, or further back
To that with eyes and claws and scales and beak.

You grip the wheel, following dotted lines:
No traffic and yet you keep to your lane.
A tic could throw your lighted world out of gear,
The heath erupt into all that has been there.

KONA MACPHEE

Kona Macphee was born in London and grew up in Melbourne, Australia. After school she moved to Sydney, where she was a music student, an apprentice motorbike mechanic, and a clerk with the Australian Bureau of Statistics. She took degrees in Robotics and Digital Technology and Computer Science at Monash University. She then moved to the University of Cambridge, where she took an M.Sc. in Computer Science. She now lives in a small village near Newmarket and works as a Web Architect in Cambridge's 'Silicon Fen'. She began writing seriously in 1997 since when she has won a number of poetry prizes including an Eric Gregory Award.

Kona Macphee has in a remarkably short time become one of the strongest new figures in British poetry. With such a range of styles, it is difficult to tell which voice, if any, she will settle on, but one suspects that the exuberant lyrical voice of 'Terminus' and 'Paul's Epiphany' is her way forward, while in 'Waltz', she has created a jewel of a poem, not one word out of place.

Paul's Epiphany

Here in the marshes, next to where
the town is moored, a noose of light
ensnares her ring

and Paul, the sharp-eyed, motors off
across the knee-deep shallows, stalls
above her, shocked to find awry
the fragile calibrations of
a living thing;

he rolls her, gently, with a foot
as if she dreams amid the mire
and might be woken, raises silt
that veils her skin

in cloudiness, her face a hint
of bones in checkmate, broken rules
beyond his ken –

and as he dangles, dumbly, there
the skin of water over her
suddenly is fleshed with pores:
a mist of rain

is falling, blurs her colours blue
and grey. Paul stands, and barely breathes,
and feels his childhood hazing out
as if a stain

is spreading, now, to saturate
the porous paper of his heart
through every vein,

and wonders if each fragile stitch
that seams the drizzled sky to ground
will hold the strain.

Terminus

A raven's restless mechanism
ticks on the signal box. Below,
midday sinuates the sheets of air
that work their quavering mesmerism,
dazing the land to stillness. Here
beside the fenceline's silted flow,

wheatstalks perpendict the lines
whose rusting railtops flash quick bronze
with flicking skinks, the sleepers, stones,
slowly weathering beneath them. Signs
have lost their lettering, blank as bones.
A peppercorn tree, some kurrajongs,

slip their roots beneath the rails
and scatter leaves and shadows. Boles
that brace the sky-flecked roof are scored
with tracks of borers, spiralled trails
that dwindle, disappear, record
a distant passage. Quick patrols

of ants dissect a fallen moth,
freighting it piecewise down the run
of pheromones that won't outlast
their usefulness. Green overgrowth
lies heavily, like something cast
to drip and dry in midday sun.

Perspective's engine hauls the eyes
along the single gauge, the groove
of jumbling rocks, which slant toward
a station hidden past the sliced
horizon. Here, no train to board.
The hot air shimmers. Nothing moves.

Waltz

He grips the gather of her waist
and pours her like a ewer into dance.
The blacklist swells of bust and bustle
brim with white-laced imminence –

her body, known by sortilege
alone, its volumes undisclosed,
tonight approximately gauged
through darkness and their civil sleeping-clothes.

Last Night at the Conference

Midnight. His expertise absently orbits the mole on her left
    breast.
Large and irregular. Bad news. She should get it checked out.
Nearly the colour and size of her nipple, it squats like a small
    troll
over her heart. As her doctor he'd order a biopsy – but he
isn't her doctor. He won't look at the rest of her, can't
look at her thighs or the wet curl of her crotch, at her face
strange as the currency furled in his wallet. The snare of the
    snub mole
captures his eye: it's the one thing he can medicalize.

Only this morning, the mole was a region uncharted in known
    space.
Somehow, this evening, the universe seems to be spiralling
    round it,
vortexed by gravity; whole worlds are about to fall in.
Paranoid now, he is whirled by irrational fears that his own wife
felt every slip of his hand, glide of his tongue, felt the harsh
thrust as his blind infidelity broke through the skin of their
    shared fate,
loosened the seals on the future. He shivers abruptly, then lies
    still,
tries not to breathe, like a man struck by a snake who attempts
slowing the flow of the poison by slowing the beat of his
    shocked heart.

Better to be in his own room, where it's quiet and still?
Dressing his body, he's dressing the wounds of this night, but
    he won't seal
arteries pumping his old life to the air with a kiss;
nor will his surgeon's articulate fingers be able to slice out
tumorous falsehood or trim lies from the truth: he's a man

too much aware of himself, or too little.

I'm going.

The door clicks.

Out in the hallway, he finds that his knees start to shake,
    puts his arm out,
thinks he can see on his skin, faintly, the stain of a mole.

Year Nine

for J.R.

Eight years the particles of virus drifted
within the bounds of his blinded eye.
We waited, hoped; the doctors' crystal
balls were masked in a wash of white.
Year Nine brought snow, and the winter light
leavened the loosened sky that piled
on roofs and branches. We exhaled
condensing residues of breath that veiled
our visions, and our presciences failed –

yet who could guess that a ball of snow
so innocently thrown, might glance against
his healthy eye, and wake the virus there?
The following day, that stricken eye rose
to an ominous dawn, a spreading flush of red
that stained the white, foretold the rise
of viral ascendancy in sky-blue eyes.

Steadily, that ice-sharp year, the virus
tightened its milky blinkers round
his sight. The dimness gradually condensed
until, on the dregs of a pallid autumn,
the winter settled in, solidified the dark.
The doctors put aside their needles and their doubts;
our tunnel vision's last light coldly faded out.
By then we were frozen, and our icicle hearts
shattered in that winter's terminating blow:
his memory of white in the cold sting of snow.

Melbourne, evening, summertime –

the flies settling, passing the torch
of insect purpose to moths, mosquitoes
(the night shift's proletariat); the sun
now tucking in until the morning, furling
the eucalpyt linen of clean blue ranges
to its chin; the murmured benedicite
of late sea breezes to the exorcized heat;

and we, alone on lawns, or jointly laid
in the mitred corners of urban parks,
curled in deckchairs, swingchairs, armchairs,
rocked on bayside boats, or dieselling home
on end-of-workday tractors as the mendicant sky
sums up its last small change of sun,

we find our warmth in evening's cool,
see drawn like sweat our gentlest selves,
are loosed to float on the slow emotions
stirred by twilight and the rightness of things.

Ice

I

Cold blue morning. Tiles of ice are laid

with perfect fit to puddles, frost
unhides the webs that chill-curled spiders made.

The tiny spikes on prickleweeds are flossed
with water crystals, grasses dusted
white with weather; footprints are embossed

along the path where treading broke the crusted
membrane of the night. Afloat
and lambent, fragile particles are mustered

to dance the clouds of breath that clear my throat.
Sunrise slices like a blade
and severed hoarfrost flecks my overcoat.

II

On promising evenings the weatherman said
the night would be freezing, so just before bed,
every winter, once or twice,
we filled a saucer and hoped for ice.

Every winter, once or twice,
We filled a saucer and hoped for ice.

We never had sleet, we never had snow,
and frost was rare and quick to go,
but every winter, once or twice,
we filled a saucer and hoped for ice.

Every winter, once or twice,
We filled a saucer and hoped for ice.

And early next morning we'd check the saucer
And always find it was filled with water,
yet every winter, once or twice,
we filled a saucer and hoped for ice.

Every winter, once or twice,
We filled a saucer and hoped for ice.

III

Through years as blue as sea-ice, striped
with white-thick scars (the cracks that healed
unevenly), observe the scene:

the schoolbag, gymslip, spider plant
still green (that browned before Grade Two
and died), the Snoopy toy, the puzzle

pieces garbled round the floor,
the halflight seeping through the gap
between the frame and drawn-to door,

the cheeks crushed in his cane-toad hand
to mouth a goldfish 'o' (a pout
for him to push his fat prick through):

a picture under glass. And now
a season's silence runs its course.
The sun has risen. Start the thaw.

Hugh's Boomerang

A haze of eucalyptus oil
in sun-fermented vapour dazes
khaki trees to blue

and lubricates the air; a hunting
boomerang slips through it, winging
skew as a drunken fruit-bat,

its barely slowing *whuh whuh whuh*
two coarse-thewed copter blades come loose.
A hunter's lethal spiral

is spun here to a tourist's toy
skimming the foreign green of trees
that know a leaner sun.

(O land of subtle colours, land
of larger air, you cannot catch:
I was not cleanly thrown.)

Hortus Botanicus

The bees in bands of honey-brown and black
thrum from wood-walled boxes, rumble back

like a pollen train, haul after yellow haul,
to the work concealed behind the beehive walls.

The Hortus rings the beehives like a garland
and no bee ventures further, to the Holland

Theatre, shrugs its polychrome array
to strip grey pollen from the grey bouquet

that's held by the girl in the wedding dress,
a grey star stitched to her white left breast.

What need have bees to plague the pale bride
who bears her own plague-mark, there on her left side,

when downstairs, out, and back along the road,
the daffodils bow beneath their shocking gold?

*The Amsterdam Hortus Botanicus is found on Plantage
Middenlaan, just down from the Holland Theatre, deportation
point for Amsterdam Jews in 1942–44 and now a Jewish war
memorial and historical museum.*

My People

my people
pass through gardens untouched by the toxic pollen of lilies
sway with the pre-factored rhythm of skyscrapers flexing in
    strong wind
thicken the air at night clubs and bus stops and cab ranks with
    their absence

my people
speak with the voices of ten million leaves, of earthquakes and
    dust motes
feed on starlight and moonshine and fallen crumbs of consumed
    dreams
grow with the vegetable fierceness of beansprouts, knowing that
    no growing is death

when they come
outracing planes whose snail trails silver the hollow sphere of
    the air
from earth where coal can burn twenty years in an underground
    seam
by sea, with sodium fire in their radiant lungfuls of water

their hands
will greet me with gestures that flux into silent legions of
    butterflies
will bear astounding weight with the sevenfold strength of ants
will move over me like perfect maggots purging the flesh of
    wounds

my people
are moving somewhere, trailing in wakes of their purpose the
    seasons
are wrung by an appetite gnawing at glaciers and atoms and bricks
are tirelessly looking for me, but in the wrong house, or country,
    or century

ROBERT SEATTER

Robert Seatter studied English at Oxford University, following which he worked as EFL teacher, actor, and in publishing. He now lives in London and works at the BBC. His poems have been widely published in magazines and have won prizes in many competitions, including commendations in the National Poetry Competition in both 1997 and 1999.

Robert Seatter's poems are painterly poems: their resonance lies largely in the juxtaposition of mood and image. The images are stark, sudden, richly colourful, often conflicting (the orange on blue in 'On Reseeing *Jules et Jim*'; the blue on orange in 'Learning Happiness'; 'Travelling to the Fish Orchards' with its "cruel silhouette against a red-gold wall"). The effect is to add texture to the narrative; the result is poetry of particular vividness.

Learning Happiness

I tell her the rules of the game
when all the coloured counters are lost –
just an empty box remains.

I tell her it is learnt like everything:
notes on a recorder, tables one to ten,
the days of the week in French.

I tell her it has witnesses: postcard,
Post-it, fax. You hold the words in place
with drawing pins on a noticeboard,

or litmus paper on litmus paper,
hang them against the window to dry –
this is the colour it has.

I tell her it is caught unawares,
a zoom lens straight to the heart:
this sudden blue balloon rising

in the seven o'clock orange of the sky,
serene and lovely as silence
above the long grey road.

Water Tank

It is cool like a church in my parents' bedroom
and above it is the water tank up in the loft – which must be
God. He speaks in bubbles. He floats like the ball cock.

And sometimes – when someone is using the bathroom –
it's as if there is water all down the wall.
And I think that must be what kindness is like,
as it flows, as it falls, as it comes in a wave.

And sometimes too, I mouth words from hymns,
there in the dark: *Abide with me, Jesu lover of my soul.*
I tell him about the way it is, inside the days,
walking on my shadow. Then I fly through the rooms

in my flailing pyjamas – with barn owl wings, with X-ray eyes,
watching my feathers glide to the ground, like splashes of paint,
like snow – the way it falls . . .

                            on my father's cufflinks
winking golden on the dressing table, a pile of coins
for the morning bus, the silence of shoes, my sister's guitar –
its long neck straining. Till everything is covered,

and God gurgles in the cistern. He makes a weight of water
to hold the roof down, stops the doors and windows
from unlocking, banging, flying away.

Penelope

The toes were not like his, nor the blunt, prodding
fingers. Nor that probing tongue that left her lips
wet. The other had kissed so neatly.

When he strayed from her side, he got lost
in the corridors, called the cook the doctor,
and mistook the postman for a landscape gardener.

Wandering into the kitchen garden he found
the abandoned beehives, hammered the slats back
one by one, then wove white willow switches

into a living rustic seat, twisted and rustled
the leaves above her head – making pergolas, arbours,
new-fangled gazebos. Never spoke of leaving.

She gave herself one, two, three months
to grow bored of him; to decide to denounce him;
to resume her walks along the beach,

peering short-sightedly out at the sea,
listening for the prow of a boat against the sand.
But instead she watched his hands

day by day with fascination. She marvelled increasingly
at their apt dexterity, as he laid strips of putty
on the rotting window frames,

cut and rehung the warped, wooden shutters
so they ceased to bang at night and dimmed,
as she slept, the sound of the sea.

Travelling to the Fish Orchards

We all want the stories.
Why that church was built there, why that island
abandoned – the banana plants and palm trees making
half the arc of a path through the botanical garden
past the glass houses.

We want the names too, the facts, the dates:
his cruel silhouette against a red-gold wall, the sleeve
all flowers, his name that sounds like aubergine.
Then the map of the family, the years in a line –
like railway stations with someone always waiting,
hat in hand on the platform,
who will say at the breakfast table later
That was where we went . . . then there.

But there are times when we take off our glasses,
enjoy myopia: lights blur, the bay is a roaring mouth,
the delicate tower a slim golden finger,
gargoyles' lips are wide brass trumpets,
a flagpole the long, twisted horn of a unicorn
vanishing down an alley.

Or we stumble on words and make strange monsters
out of translation – like the time I grew peaches then fishes
out of the milk-green canals of an island.
The men traipsed their feet through the thick, damp
    undergrowth,
waited under trees in abandoned valleys
for the golden scales to shine.

On Reseeing *Jules et Jim*

In middle age, unreal middle age –
years like snow, the soft and silent stealth
of their covering – I wake without love,

sheets adrift, lines of clear, white light
through the blind. Wake too with a sense
of having learnt content, a here-and-now content,

a ceasing of the raging – oranges balanced
against the blue of the table top, spherical,
poised, knowing their weight. Then, outside,

a tree taps light branches on the window,
fingers on a memory drum, and those moments
burn back untouchable behind glass, make

a gesture of sound, a something untranslatable.
These are the days when an old film forces tears,
absolutes steadfast against passing trains, clouds, a river,

all those black and white faces waiting for colour.

Pumpkins

We are talking about what we will do in this Hallowe'en city.
The last day of October and everyone mad for it;
even the airport staff wear cat masks, witches' hats, dangling
    spiders,
smile their efficiency toothlessly, clap each other on the back
at bigger, better costumes. Outside, San Francisco gleams
and preens itself – knife-edge shadows of fire-escapes on the wall,
cats walking softly on warm, warm air. I wonder if my skin
is some sort of disguise. You sing under your breath *where has
all the fog gone?* In the streets of the Castro the gay crowds muster:
seven identical 1940s sailor girls – one chucks me under the chin,
calls me *darlin', loverboy, sexy*; duos of Dorothys replete with Toto
in a basket; a tottering Carmen Miranda who keeps giving away
her fruit, some of it real, some of it not. You bite into bright red
    plastic.
One white-frocked Marilyn Monroe stands over a heating grill,
the pleats of her skirt waiting for the moment. From your room
in the Mission – cool, grey, a painting of a monkey model
    (armless)
and a blue toy car on the wall – we watch your friend Louis
at the opposite window, carving his pumpkin, heaping the flesh
in a pale orange mound to one side, cutting out a smile,
gap-toothed, triangular. It stares back out at us,
laughter in its throat. Later, Louis paints his face in the mirror,
slips on the thin, black skin of a dress. It glitters and shimmers
inside the window, departing leaves us mirrorless, empty.
We keep on talking about what we will do in this Hallowe'en city,
how to be a part of it, how we'd cut the pumpkin we might buy,
hack the curve of its lips. Switching the light off,
we conjure its taste, tongue our smiles in the gaps in between.

Hipsters

The trying them on was of course
the most embarrassing:
that struggle of zips and shoelaces in a drafty cubicle,
and my mother's too loud, too middle-class voice
asking *Are you ready?*, as she
twitched the curtain.

And the smirk of the assistant, of an age
to be at school with me, as I explained
with a truculence that I knew sounded peevish,
that these were not really hipster enough.
And no, I didn't want the grey flannels
or the lovat green tweeds.

What I wanted, I knew, with total single-mindedness,
was purple hipsters
like Jeremy Slater's in the fifth year,
adding murderously under my breath
a list of other essential needs:
brown button boots,
a black crushed velvet jacket,
sideburns, a Frank Zappa moustache,
a 150 cc moped, the latest Led Zeppelin album,
a girlfriend with a name like Pen or Jade or Lisa,
a lost virginity, a divorced parent,
a hollow-eyed drug problem
and a near successful suicide.

But it being Wednesday and half-day closing,
I was lucky to get
even the purple hipsters.

Boy Blue

Was it a taste for fashionable narcolepsy, this dropping down
breathless in the hay? Crumpling his bright blue
corduroy, forgetful of his lump of cheese and white square
of bread, water bottle hissing its silver contents

into corn dust. The sheep went wild and random, nibbling at
raggedy hillsides as they struggled over stiles, splashed down
ditches and rootled in waste-paper bins. Three of them died.
In the valley, the village expected his horn from before
    midday,

waited for its blunt-nosed sound to come pushing through
the warm afternoon; were puzzled instead by silence.
But guessed that he must have gone farther over the hill, recalled
his busy list of tickable achievements: *Things to do before*

20, 30, 40. So they listened to the weather forecast,
drank dark brown tea and stroked the cat – not knowing that
    morning
he had woken perturbed, had stared at the clock
with no recognition in his eyes, had stood in the bathroom

and felt affinity only with the blind bar of soap . . . washed away
in cold clear water. Later in the grass he had watched,
near his eyelash, a silent ant climbing jungles of lines,
had heard the earth turning mysterious under his head,

had realized there were suits of more than one colour.

Pumpkin Summer

No rain for two weeks
and the pumpkins grow rampant in the July sun:
shiny, orange footballs lolling on the earth.
The garden shrinks.

The Italian lodger sleeping in the spare room
looks dubious at their growing,
walks around the house practising the word –
pumpkin, pumpkin.

He forgets it the next day, goes out
to fuck boys in the baked Oxford meadows,
observes the pumpkin progress
with a face like guilt, eyebrows in a line.

He phones home to his papa and fidanzata:
I love it here: the colleges, the history...
yes, I miss you too. But my English
is improving – I will stay longer.

Later in the moonlight, he lies wide awake,
feels every globe swelling:
a sheen of expectation, root like a claw.
The bedroom walls shrink.

He leaves me tearfully – to go back to Milan,
his suitcases full of English Breakfast Tea;
insists on one last visit to look at the monster.
Pumpkin, pumpkin, he mouths in silence.

In another week, I cut the stalks,
lay the heavy, orange flesh on the draining board.
The lawn lies reclaimed,
tame as a living room carpet.

Family Affair

Your brothers, sisters, divorced parents and animals,
an aunt in Brazil, a cousin expert on the Italian Mafia –
the fact of it was, I fell in love with you all.
For punk hair, pregnancies, Pater and pubes
discussed with volubility at the breakfast table.
For the talent you all had of discovering indiscretions
like the clonk of a plastic toy from a bumper crisp bag,
of winkling truth out with flamboyancy and thoroughness,
writing it with a silver aerosol across the air. Later,
there would be someone with a dustpan and brush,
there would be kindness on wide trays dispensed
from the kitchen: doorsteps of sandwiches oozing Marmite
and peanut butter, mugs with indecent mottos all full
of steaming tea. Liked too the fact that your family car
wasn't clean, but autographed with mud, full of theatre props
and wellingtons, that your dog was called 'dog'
and the plants in your garden had no label, no name,
that you had bedrooms on the ground floor, a living room
at the top, and your brother kept his python periodically
in the bath – frightening the girlfriends, the boyfriends
who turned up, with never a shortage of milk for breakfast.
That you made me feel I was as easy as you, as brilliant,
as funny, as shot through with laughter, that the windows
in my house were open like yours, glittering with light
and interesting laundry. Not surprising, I suppose,
that you returned the compliment, that you longed for
my family's yards of clean table cloth, its careful breath
of politeness, rooms of space; for the dozing Sunday silence
broken intermittently by the bark of a dog called Rover.

First Marriage

Looking back, it seemed to happen
underwater. The shoes were smaller,
the hands quite white, the voices came back
in bubbles like raspberries: I do, I do.

Did I? Did we somewhere make those lists,
pick a tie to match your bouquet (eau de nil
not jade; we go through every shade of green),
smile for a mantlepiece across swimming rooms,

buy curtain rings and tin openers,
make love in front of a silent TV (our bodies
striped in watery light) and realize at night
that the breathing goes on forever –

each exhalation like a wave? Water
on our chests in a grey and green column
as far as we could see. So we swam
to the surface, clambered onto the mantlepiece,

then watched the furniture float slowly away.

At Central Station, Milan

The great arch of it. A cathedral of glass
where no bells swing. Only the incantation
of name on name, whispered at windows:

Roma, Firenze, Pavia, Bergamo.
I pay you for otherness, for perhaps –
for the feel of earth sliding under my feet,

for the words I fling in handfuls
into your space like a lung. To breathe
the definitions of finish, which makes

a something of uncountable continuation,
second on second of it. Which makes
a something against the rush of leaves,

the fence poles that flicker and fidget
at my eye, the pale hanging face that might be
mine out there on the window, on the night.

JULIAN TURNER

Julian Turner was born in Cheadle Hulme, near
Manchester, in 1955. His poetry has been published
in magazines including *The Rialto* and *Verse*, and has
benefited from the support and criticism of Michael
Donaghy, Ian Duhig and Paul Farley. In 1999 he col-
laborated with artist Alison Rouse on *Loanwords*, an
art-box containing poems and etchings. He lives with
his partner and daughter in Otley, West Yorkshire,
and works as chief executive of Leeds Mind.

Describing himself as 'always a slow starter', Julian
Turner writes poems which display a degree of crafts-
manship and confidence exceptional for a poet yet to
publish his first collection. Turner is equally at home
with the comic ('Leg the Dentist') and the tragic (the
moving, yet admirably unsentimental 'Tennis Ball'),
while his ability in sustaining narrative is exemplified
in the masterly 'Kintaro Grows Old'.

Schubert

It shocked me Schubert liked to lie all day
in bed with his huge wolfhound, Valkyrie,
and maybe Liz his girlfriend too. He played

violin in three orchestras and fiddle in
a scratch washboard outfit, ska and skiffle on
Fridays, the rest of his week spent between

the bed and front room mending instruments.
He'd stroke an Amati of doubtful provenance
to life to conjure me its resonance.

Sometimes he had to stash the shop sign when
the Revenue called up. He'd grin, his wine
silver in his hand, his thin lips carmine.

On Sundays he would shepherd me to the Lord
Napier to hear Big Bill Broonzy, loud,
with the smoky sixths and laid-back weekend crowds.

I was young then and London was a blur
of rain, demolished tower blocks and beer.
I spent the nights with him and Frank, a software

freak, saying how we'd died: Schubert at eight
lying in darkness, face to the wall, a blanket
of hessian dyed to block the window out,

called back from the burning light by his dad,
to no sight or sound for several months; Frank dead
four minutes in the crash; all of us glad

to get a second chance, three of the 'twice-born'
talking away the extra time in Thorn-
ton Heath, waiting for the ordinary light of dawn.

Against Flowers

after Ciaran Carson

Sowbane, Bogwort, Bugloss, Toadflax and Forget-me-not:
it will be the detritus of these I will scrape from my boots
    at dusk,
coming home from the valley decked out like Florizel, slightly
perspiring, having pitched the fury of my feet against all manner
of harmless thing, against the pert, cross-clashing blades
    of grass,
their lethal edges steel in the glistening dew, against the dreamy
    stars
of wild garlic floating in the forest's deep twilight, small boats
upon a sea in which all nightmares lurk, against the innocent
    and mild,
the mindless daffodil, the insulting abundance of the buttercup,
the ox-eye's wink, the retributive, infuriating non-amnesia of
    poppies,
against even leaf-mould and the lichens whose modest
    encrustations
have taken centuries to build, simply because of their close
    kinship,
in short, against everything which reminds me of you.
And if we must communicate, we will do so through Interfauna.

Bert Haines' Yard

What was it my dad and brother were searching for
those times they dragged me down to Bert Haines' yard,
thistles and groundsel bushing up through floors
of cars, the unhinged gravestones of van doors
tilting towards the sun, their paintwork scarred
by unrecorded accidents, a ghost
topography where all things come to rest,

the stripped down bicycles and engine parts,
vast sprockets from the giants' industries,
their magnitude remembering lost arts
of universes smelted and cast in foundries
moving at night to patterns planned by star charts,
an afterlife of objects grassed in dust
and grease, a leaf-soft mall which sells what's lost,

forgotten, repossessed, passed on: cement
statues, wheelless wheel barrows, old machines,
their movements gone? Maybe some link between
two boyhoods, a chain broken by accident
which they must mend but didn't have the means?
To find among the litter of the dead
a golden circlip? Neither ever said.

Reportage

Later, among the rubble roads of the suburbs
where already the broken slabs were being craned,
the iron rods uncased from them like ribs –
rebuilding was in the air, a kind of season –

I was allowed to meet a small huddle of children,
some of them mute and some merely silent
as if on parade, all with the same desiccated
exhalation coming from their throats.

After some afternoons in the unplastered classroom
they were able to speak words. They hadn't wanted this,
they were still small and only wanted to meet
their parents soon, please, or scream in the park.

Further in, where gutted windows raised their eyebrows
and whole streets were sealed in with a black tar,
others played jackstraws with the fingerbones
on a sticky step. They lifted their shirts to scars

thin as their smiles. They made reloading actions,
rituals to ward off a *once-upon-a-time*
when they had filled schools with shouted insults
and lusted over labels they would have killed for.

More of it, more, they said, wiping the rainwater
from unblinking eyes, watching with disinterest
the cablemen in trucks, the smiling orderlies
waiting at the street end to rope them together.

Nearer the centre silence had turned on itself.
Three small girls sat on a manicured lawn.
I joined them on the grass to wait, the sun
kindly warming the back of my old shirt.

Gone midnight: *You were expected*, one said,
What took you so long? Sit-down-and-then-move-on,
that's what you're called, or Come-to-count-the-dead;
your kindness isn't necessary here.

Her smile broke below unclouded eyes.
It grew into a knot around her neck.
Several small skulls watched from up a tree
as if expecting something more of me.

I kicked my heels with other journalists.
I filed my copy through the ears of stone.
I was alone with those I could not tell
about the city, which is everyone.

Penalty of Stroke and Distance

These are the ones whose rules, exact and pure,
remind you poor conditions are no excuse,
who in all weathers will turn out and draw
their pitching irons cold from rusted pools,
who practise after dark their follow-through,
their swing-weight, wrist cock and pre-putt routine
alone with fog or rain in motley shoes
like shadows on the ninth at Hallowe'en.

Have you seen them when snow has turned the links
into a glittercloth of blinding stymies?
Then they cut loose, lost on the fairway banks,
intent and abstract, caddying their dead ponies
through waistdeep drifts across Antarctica.
They shield their faces from the icy sun
in search of pitchmarks on a glacier,
in search of the most extreme hole-in-one.

You must have seen them, in the dead afternoon
returning with their far-off eyes, as touched
as if they were illuminated from within,
the long climb over and their summit reached,
their parka hoods on fire; forgotten ones
who stumble home, their hair as white as snow,
to strangeness at the heart of what they know,
uncomprehending faces, eyes which shun.

The Director's Cut

The hands that use the knife are not my own.
The way the flesh peels back like parted lips,
the way the walls of tissue raspberry-ripple,
sudden shocks of rush in little sips,
the pinching of the skin to stem the blood,
the numbness spreading through the musculature,
the way the knife lies by the plate of toast,
the linen dressings creamy, clean and sure;

like being in a fight with no one else,
exact and under my control, the tense
build-up, the downjerk of the hand, the surge
of quick relief; the stupid, dull attempts
to mend it; wet, red cloths, the winding round
of bandages; the hush. All these make sense.

Kintaro Grows Old

When young I scarcely knew my size or strength,
a cub of bears who couldn't have their own:
their shaggy natures lent me mammal-sense,
the tang of fear and how to stand alone,
to match brute force with wit, muscle for muscle
in the dense busks and stubbings, taught me how deep
all habits run, the parts still animal
which have their honour and define our scope.

My gift was chasing on the heels of fright.
The truth is, I doubted I was strong.
I thought my body frail, my build slight.
Much later when I had to face the gang,
take in their looks and sniff their reek of fear,
I was surprised at such a simple thing –
that bullying or going off to war
would stop if terror could sit still and sing.

There comes a time all giants learn their size.
It takes ages for this knowledge to evolve,
as if the body was a crude disguise
which slows the truth or makes it hard to prove.
Some find it in the fear in people's faces,
others in comments lovers make at night
confessing comfort in our curl-up places.
I found out mine when age began to bite.

The costs of size: a body's second skin,
its milky softness changed to salmon scales;
the sinews tightening like hawsers when
I stood to stretch at dawn; fir-trunk ankles;
eye-clouding mists; the noise of old machines –
the heart's pump heave, the punctured bellows wheeze,
their leather sides tattooed with ropes of veins –
from all of these I learnt how huge I was.

I know that I may not refuse my fate:
the symbol of a courage scarcely felt
to frighten children, urge them on to fight,
a woodland hulk which bears and combat built,
a smiling oaf to keep the thieves from meat,
a Mr Sturdy Oak. I'm none of these,
just one small son his parents couldn't beat.
May God prevent the strengthening of boys.

Kintaro, in Japanese folklore, was a feral child who went on to free Edo (modern Tokyo) from a terrorizing band of thugs. He is celebrated during Children's Day.

The Magnificent History of the English

My aunt has cooked me four lamb chops for tea.
She waves the mint sauce. Like a magician
she stands in strip-light clenching and unclenching
her freckled, arthritic hands on empty air.

Together, we have trawled through the photo albums
and found Ida – the great aunt I remember
shrunk beside the fireplace in Hitchin, half-hidden
by the tallboy, her hands afraid like birds.

But in these tiny snaps she's young again,
even happy-looking. Here she is with Bud –
her pet name for my aunt – her rusty, damaged
blade of a face suddenly lit from within.

She was how my aunt survived the cold
touch of her own mother who only saw her son,
who lavished love on him, the boast of Arlesey
at her bridge parties, and who gave her none.

Towards the end of Ida's album Tom
appears, his bland disguise of tennis whites
conceals his marriedness, the way he had
her in the potting shed, the fists of his knees,

and other men: the Revd. Knightly in
the bucket seat of 'the good old Morris Cowley',
tennis with doctors from the loony bin,
and Cecil Soundry shaving in his vest.

On the inside back cover Bud stands
squinting up at the sun. She holds a wand
of bracken. With her other arm she looks
for Ida who bends down to fill her hand.

My aunt carries out the bones. She locks
the door on distant memory with relief.
We both look down the long corridor, and laugh
at the fucked Turners, English as roast beef.

Tennis Ball

All things have gravity – its universal
principal makes Earth come up to meet
a tennis ball; the lover bearing down
provokes a rise; the rails push up against
the train and parachutists spread themselves
like fingers on a fountain-flail of air
until their ribbon snakes up to the clouds;
fledglings fall from nests to find their wings;
a foal is dropped and climbs on to his feet;
the Fall implies a faith in being caught.
Such things have weight.
Jane tied a brief knot in a nylon rope,
climbed up into an open loft and dipped,
a swallow from a wire. She just hung there.

Leg the Dentist

All pain is finite, dentists say.
My room-sized tongue is pinned by her
spare thumb. She tamps down drums of clay
and cotton-wool. I ng and urr.

Her bone-white fingers rummage in
the soft soil of my face, poking
down for Yorick with a tiny
fork and spade, and she's not joking

as she banters to the nurse
who's shlopping up the ready-mix.
She leans on me, her rose lips pursed.
You only get this close in sex:

I'll pay for this. The hole half-dug
she muses gravely what to do
while we can both hear drifting up
through silence, Hell's Radio 2.

SARAH WARDLE

Sarah Wardle was born in London in 1969. She read Classics at Lincoln College, Oxford and English at the University of Sussex, where she is now doing her doctorate. She won the Geoffrey Dearmer Prize, *Poetry Review*'s New Poet of the Year Award, in 1999. Recordings of her reading from her own work have been featured on ArtsOnline.com.

Sarah Wardle's poetry is informed by a love of classics and philosophy, by the politics of love affairs, university, travel, health and home. Her light, formal style and love of rhyme are set against a hint of darkness and a wicked wit. 'Word Hill' and 'Age of Awareness' show her skill at building up incantatory lists, while her penchant for playful sonnets, pithy fragments as well as longer sustained pieces show an impressive range for such a singular voice.

Arcadia

As if a country kitchen were where we sat
and you wore a smock, and I an apron,
as I rocked a newborn asleep in his cot,
while through the door came laughter from our other children,

and this table, instead of papers and books,
held a jug of ale and a weekly wage,
while the scent of baked ham spread as it cooked,
and with one hand I stirred in onion and sage,

I caught you lift your straggling thoughts over a fence,
your face framed offguard, gazing fields away,
as you herded your words into a sentence,
your eyes brown and deep as the soil's clay.

To the Reader

The words I write become another world,
where I am both the poem and the maker,
the creator, who decides what light is called,
and the *logos*, which is uttered by the speaker,
and in this place virtual love is possible,
and for the best in a parallel universe,
and happens on a planet the size of a pebble,
when you and I invisibly move the earth,
but this poem is only one of many
amid all the pages lost on library shelves,
and that planet revolves round an infinity
of other worlds and other people's selves,
and my pebble lies with millions on the beach,
where you might choose it, then skim it out to sea.

Young Man in Bronze

The young man slouches his weight on one leg,
propping up an imaginary bar which serves
retsina in pint glasses.
You get the feeling he spent last night
profaning the mysteries,
and mutilated some statues on the way home.

This is the artist at his most provocative.
He had a preference for this model,
used to vie to be the one
to anoint him with oils down at the club,
got badly into debt at some point,
because of the lad's appetite for horses.

He cast the features lovingly,
laid the victor's laurel on his head like a halo,
didn't miss a detail,
not a curl, not a muscle. You can see
youth's arrogance in the tilt of his face.
His whole body bursts with potential movement.

When Greece became a province,
he was flogged as booty to a dealer in Rome,
who sold him off to a senator.
He was given pride of place in the atrium,
alongside marble busts of the ancestors,
and was much admired by guests.

Today he stands in a museum,
daring tourists to avert their eyes,
like a pop star on his pedestal.
I run my fingers over his body,
but where there should be warmth,
the bronze is cold.

Word Hill

Not a hill built on words
torn from dictionaries, nor absurd
words with Latin stems,
nor Russian, nor Arabic, none of them.

Not a burial mound of archaisms,
of words with obsolete definitions,
nor a dig where archaeology
finds ostracisms on pottery.

Not a tip of Coke cans, baked bean tins,
train tickets, newsprint, magazines,
nor a land raise of verbal waste,
which villagers protest against.

Not a hillside tomb to Shakespeare's works,
nor stockpiled copies of a thesaurus.
Not the place where the gallows stand
on a blackboard in games of Hangman.

Not a bank of crossword clues,
one down, two across, none of those,
nor a stack of all the words
you could possibly have on a Scrabble board.

Not a hilltop fort, where tongues competed
and the losing language was translated,
nor the far-off peak where madmen go
to let their speech drift down like snow.

Only a Birmingham cul-de-sac,
like a needle hidden in a haystack,
where two girls freewheel down the street
sometime in nineteen seventy-eight.

Age of Awareness

Catkin days and hedgerow hours
fleet like shafts of chapel sun.
Childhood in a cobwebbed bower
guards a treasure chest of fun.

By the lake a fabled tower
vouches for a virgin nun.
In the vale a farmer glowers.
Smoke is rising from his gun.

Crimson and vermilion flowers
taint white beds of alyssum.
In the pail the milk turns sour.
Fairytales repeat the pun.

The defence declines to cower
when the time for truth has come.
The trick is sharing out the power
once the battleground is won.

Sceptic's Song

after Montale

I fear one day, as I walk down the street,
I shall see through the window of the world.
Looking over my shoulder, my eyes will meet
a void, no drunk's vision, but a vacant whirl.

Then reality will vanish, the reel turn
and illusion again be projected on
all nothingness, but in me the truth will burn,
for I'll know that I too am part of the con.

Reading Room Requiem

Suppose a poet had been last to leave
the Reading Room, the final cell to die
in the giant brain that enclosed the eye
of its great domed mind, had been first to receive

the impression of the pews of learning
sitting empty, the god of knowledge gone,
fled through a hole, as in the Pantheon,
shelves raided, books stacked as if for burning,

suppose he'd seen all this and then, turning,
had shrugged and walked out beneath the golden orb
of the British Museum, quite absorbed
in imagination with ideas churning,

detached as Nero declaiming a song
of Troy's destruction as Rome blazed,
men torched monuments, temples were razed,
suppose him cold-hearted as he went along,

but picture him warmed by a current of thought,
pausing trivially to feel the heat
from hot chestnut coals in Great Russell Street,
pleased to find an image he had not sought.

Buridan's Ass

On Blackpool beach I was motivated
by carrots and sticks, easily sated
with sugar lumps from indulgent kids,
though I had my dreams. Of course I did,
wanted to bear the returned Messiah
into town, or find a big-time buyer
for a Cleopatra who bathed in pints.
Yes, *Aesop: The Movie* was in my sights.
Then I volunteered, bribed by extra cash,
for an egghead's experiment. That rash
impulse to grab the dosh and take the bait
was the last whim I had. I vacillate,
starving midway between two equal bales,
undecided as shoppers at the sales.
Now RSPCA photographers
snap me to warn of cruel philosophers.

In the National Palace Museum, Taiwan

Here in this entrepreneurial State
they work in night markets and evening school.
A Ming porcelain bowl shows Dragon Gate,
where a carp rises from a cobalt pool

to become that creature in mist above,
a symbol of strength, of the emperor,
of success – a concept these people love,
who fled from a communist conqueror.

In their port cargoes prepare to embark.
In their World Trade Centre the day's begun.
China Steel is the scale of a theme park.
Textile factory machines run and run.

But see how each busy capitalist
stares serenely through an exhibit's glass
to gaze at lotus flowers, a phoenix,
or philosophers on a mountain path.

The Close

Where do they live, the sounds of other people,
the boy who plays his trumpet out of key,
the woman talking at her kitchen table,
the snatch of a tennis match on TV,

the sprinkler on a lawn, set to stop and go,
the dog that barks whenever it is bored,
the music from a curtained upstairs window,
the wood pigeon which plays its stuck record?

Where do they live, in or outside you?
You ask till you no longer want to know,
because you can hear your own footsteps too,
and the silence of your shadow on the road.

Acknowledgements

RICHARD ARONOWITZ: 'Foetal Position' in *The Independent*; 'Snowstorm Souvenir' in *Navis*; 'New York, Fourth of July' in *The Bridport Prize Anthology 1999*.

ROS BARBER: 'Endnote' in *The Frogmore Papers*; 'Eve's Hobby', 'Well' and 'Pronoun' in *Poetry Review*; 'He'd Push My Hands Together' in *Stand*; 'The Dancer' in *The North*.

SIÂN HUGHES: 'Romance' in *The Times Literary Supplement*; 'Soap' in *Poetry Review*; 'The Sacking Offence' in *London Magazine*; 'Saltpetre', 'Secret Lives' and 'Map-Reading' in the pamphlet *Saltpetre* published by Smith/Doorstop Books.

A.B. JACKSON: 'The Christmas Pet' and 'In Memory of R.D. Laing' in *New Writing Scotland*; 'Journey' and 'Filing' in *London Magazine*; 'Stammer' has been heavily revised since its first appearance in *The Dark Horse*.

TABISH KHAIR: all poems in this selection, with the exception of '1.15 a.m.', appeared in *Where Parallel Lines Meet*, published by Penguin India, 2000.

KONA MACPHEE: 'Paul's Epiphany' and 'Year Nine' in *Acumen*; 'Terminus' in *Poetry Wales*; 'Hugh's Boomerang' and 'Three Poems' in *Reactions* anthology published by Pen & Inc.

ROBERT SEATTER: 'Travelling To the Fish Orchards' in *Ambit*.

JULIAN TURNER: 'The Magnificent History of the English' in *The Reater*; 'The Director's Cut' and 'Penalty of Stroke and Distance' in *Poetry London*; 'Tennis Ball' and 'Reportage' in *The Rialto*; 'Against Flowers' at boomerangUK.com.

SARAH WARDLE: 'In the National Palace Museum, Taiwan', 'Sceptic's Song', 'Reading Room Requiem', 'The Close' and 'To the Reader' in *Poetry Review*; 'Arcadia' and 'Young Man in Bronze' in *University of Sussex Bulletin*; 'Arcadia' also appeared in *The Times Literary Supplement*.